Questions And Answers On Bible Prophecy

by
Dr. Hilton Sutton

HARRISON HOUSE
Tulsa, Oklahoma

Unless otherwise indicated,
all Scripture quotations are taken from
the *King James Version* of the Bible.

Questions And Answers On Bible Prophecy
ISBN 0-89274-253-4
Copyright © 1982 by Hilton Sutton
Mission To America
736 Wilson Road
Humble, Texas 77338

Published by Harrison House, Inc.
P. O. Box 35035
Tulsa, Oklahoma 74135

Preface

The Church is filled with questions about Bible prophecy, particularly about the book of Revelation. Since about thirty-seven percent of the Bible is prophetic scripture, we need to have an understanding. Our faith is based on all of God's Word, not just favorite verses and passages. Therefore, the prophetic books are equally important to the believer.

All of the questions in this book have come from believers, folks just like you. Some were taken from letters written to me, while others came from people attending our seminars. I have not created any of these questions.

This is an unusual book. I believe you will be informed and edified by the material it contains. The time for understanding the Word—all of it—has come. Knowledge is now increasing and the

Church should get a lion's share of that increase. The prophet Daniel predicted the increase of knowledge (ch. 12, v. 4), so let the knowledge of God prevail over all theological traditions and arguments.

—Hilton Sutton

Questions And Answers On Bible Prophecy

Why are the prophetic books of the Bible important?

The prophetic books and their predictions are important for several reasons:

1. They are part of God's Word.

2. All Scripture is from God and profitable. (2 Tim. 3:16.)

3. Our faith must operate on the whole Word of God and be supported by it. (Rom. 10:17.)

4. They inform us of Israel's historical value, especially by relating how God dealt with His original chosen people.

5. They reveal God's plan and time-table—knowledge which the Church must have.

How did the word *rapture* come to be identified with the catching up of the Church?

Rapture means "the state of being carried away with joy, love, and pleasure, resulting in ecstasy." It is often used to replace the following biblical terms: "received of the Lord" (John 14:3), "caught up to meet the Lord" (1 Thess. 4:17), and "gathered together unto the Lord" (2 Thess. 2:1).

Upon studying the above scriptures in the context of the rest of the Bible, we discover the event to be depicted as a joyous, comforting celebration of great magnitude, a connotation which coincides with the definition of *rapture*.

Any believer can use the word *rapture* knowing that it sums up all the joy in the biblical phrases referring to that event.

Will the born-again Christians who are out of fellowship with God—those who

are lukewarm or carnal—be caught up in the Rapture?

Some controversy surrounds this very interesting question concerning the catching up of the Church. The answer, I'm sorry to say, is that they won't be.

This viewpoint is based on the story of the ten virgins in Matthew 25 and on the description of the lukewarm church in Revelation 3.

Upon careful examination of the story of the ten virgins—five wise and five foolish—you will discover that the wise went into the marriage chamber with the bridegroom. Upon studying the book of Revelation, you will discover that the marriage chamber is in heaven, not on earth. Revelation 19, beginning with verse 1, clearly establishes that the Wedding and the following Marriage Supper of the Lamb, again, take place in heaven, not on earth.

The foolish virgins had everything the wise ones had, including oil. Their lamps burned, but were going out, because they hadn't kept themselves ready for the event. The foolish virgins did not go into the marriage chamber. The wise virgins—those who were ready—did. This means that the wise virgins made it to heaven. From this we see that the Church must be taken to heaven.

Revelation 3 describes the Laodicean church which was neither hot nor cold, but lukewarm. Lukewarm Christians have lost their first love and are spiritually bankrupt. They are much the same as the foolish virgins who simply were not ready for a prophesied event. Strong statements are made about both groups. The foolish virgins did not go into the wedding chamber with the bridegroom. The lukewarm Christian is "spewed out" of the mouth of the Lord! (Rev. 3:16.)

So, you see, it is possible for a born-again believer to miss the Rapture.

However, for this to happen, one has to become careless about his daily walk with Jesus Christ and become a luke-warm Christian, unprepared for the Rapture of the Church. The foolish virgins had the same opportunities as the wise. Missing the Rapture is not equivalent to being lost, but it does mean going through part of the Tribulation.

How do we know that there will be a Rapture?

Hebrews 9:28 says, *Unto them that look for him shall he appear the second time without sin unto salvation.*

This verse clearly declares that Jesus' appearance to those who look for Him has nothing to do with sin but with finishing their salvation. The final act of their bodies becoming incorruptible, immortal, and glorified is the finished work of salvation. This will happen at Jesus' appearance as He receives the Church unto Himself. (1 Cor. 15:51-53.)

11

Jesus said, *If I go and prepare a place for you, I will come again, and receive you unto myself; that where I am, there ye may be also* (John 14:3). This statement certainly declares a change of location for Jesus' followers. He is going to take them unto Himself.

Jesus also said, *Watch ye therefore, and pray always, that ye may be accounted worthy to escape all these things that shall come to pass, and to stand before the Son of man* (Luke 21:36). Without question, this statement establishes that the followers of Jesus who are watching and praying will escape by being quickly removed from their earthly scene. They will escape all the events of the future Tribulation and stand with Jesus. By no stretch of the imagination does the word *escape* mean "to be hidden away." It means "to go quickly out from."

Consider other Bible truths which picture the Church in heaven. The Church will get to sit down in Jesus' throne as He is seated with His Father in heaven. (Rev. 3:21.) John describes the Church in heaven watching the preparation of the Wedding to be followed by the Marriage Supper of the Lamb. (Rev. 19:1-10.) The prophet Zechariah tells us that the saints return with Christ from heaven on the final day of the Tribulation. (Zech. 14:5; confirmed by Rev. 17:14 and 19:14.)

No Bible student can dispute the clear-cut picture the Bible gives of the Rapture. Do you know why? There are too many Rapture events described in the Scriptures for any honest Bible student to deny the Rapture.

Can we be certain that the Rapture of the Church takes place *before* the Tribulation?

Daniel 9:24-27 clearly reveals the exact point at which the Antichrist as Satan's agent begins his operation in relationship to the Tribulation. The Tribulation is the last seven years of God's direct work to bring all Israel back to Himself. Daniel tells us the Antichrist enters into an agreement with Israel for one week (which is seven years long). Since he enters into an agreement with Israel for one week, he has to do it at the beginning.

Daniel goes on to reveal that in the middle of that week, or after three and one-half years, the Antichrist will break his agreement with Israel. This, of course, is in the very middle of that seven-year period. From this biblical reference, we know exactly when the Antichrist will begin his activities.

Notice: the Apostle Paul writes that the Antichrist—the man of sin, the son of perdition—*may not* begin his earthly operation until *he* who has been withholding him has been taken out of the way. (2 Thess. 2:1-9.) Daniel has established when the Antichrist begins his assignment and Paul tells us the withholder of that satanic plan must be taken out of the way before the man of sin can be revealed. There is a withholder, a hindering factor, stronger than Satan.

Many Bible interpreters immediately say *he* who must be taken is the Holy Spirit. Not so! The Holy Spirit is God the Holy Ghost. Being God the Holy Ghost, He has the unique ability of being everywhere all the time and can't be taken out or put in.

If the Holy Spirit were taken from the earth, He could not operate here, and no one could be saved during that seven-year period. Paul teaches in Romans 11:25,26 that all Israel will be saved. Revelation 7:9-17 tells us that the Great Multitude will be saved during the Tribulation. Zechariah 8:23 tells us that during that same time, ten times as many Gentile men will be saved as there are Jews.

Because the Holy Spirit (Holy Ghost) is the agent of salvation, no possibility exists that He can be taken away. Since so many Jews and Gentiles are to be saved in the Tribulation, the Holy

Spirit must, of necessity, be here on earth. It is the Holy Spirit Who convicts of sin and Who testifies of Jesus. (John 16:8; 15:26.) Jesus said that all men must be drawn unto Him by the Father. (John 6:44.) Through studying the Gospel of John, we learn that the Holy Spirit is the agent through which this is accomplished.

We see from the above discussion that the Holy Spirit must remain on earth for all the Multitude to be saved. Therefore, the *he* of 2 Thessalonians 2:1-9 that must be taken out of the way can only be the Church. There is no other choice.

Some declare that the Church is not *he;* but the Church is most certainly *he.* Everybody has gotten hung up on calling the Church *she.* Probably this results from an overemphasis on the identity of the Church in relationship to Christ as a bride. By doing this, we have not considered the full identity of the Church in relationship to Jesus.

Through studying the Apostle Paul's writings, we learn that the Church is the Body of Christ, of which Christ is the Head. (See 1 Cor. 12:12-14,27; Eph. 4:16; Col. 1:18; 2:17,19; Rom. 12:4,5.) Therefore, the Church is the Body of Christ and Jesus is the Head of that Body. From this, we see that the Church cannot be identified as *she*, but as *he*—the Body of Christ. *He*, who must be removed before the Antichrist can begin his activity, is none other than the Church.

Carefully examine Revelation, chapters 4, 5, and 6.

Chapter 4 records an experience the Holy Spirit permitted John to have. John experienced the exact event described by Paul in 1 Thessalonians 4:16,17:

For the Lord himself shall descend from heaven with a shout, with the voice of the archangel, and with the trump of God: and the dead in Christ shall rise first:

17

Then we which are alive and remain shall be caught up together with them in the clouds, to meet the Lord in the air: and so shall we ever be with the Lord.

In chapters 4 and 5 we read John's description of the twenty-four elders which represent every born-again believer. John depicts this group standing with Jesus before the Father's throne. The group, or company, watch Jesus walk to the throne to take a book from His Father's hand. The book has seven seals upon it which only Jesus can open.

Chapter 6 describes the opening of the first seal. This begins the seven-year period we have been taught to call the Tribulation.

So, with the Church caught up and the first seal opened, the Antichrist begins a seven-year assignment. The Rapture is definitely before the beginning of the Tribulation.

Note: Some teach that the Church will go through all or at least part of the

Tribulation. They indicate that persecution and suffering will be the cause for the Church to watch, pray, and look for Jesus' appearing.

This negative theology does not allow for there being men and women who are doers of the Word. These believers will not be weak or fearful people; nor will they be in hiding, awaiting the Lord to just barely rescue them in time from their trouble. They will be overcoming conquerors—operators in power, love, and a sound mind—who pull down strongholds. The watching, praying, looking, and working Church will be giving Satan his due until the time that they are snatched away. Ephesians 5:27 would then be inappropriate because the Lord will present unto Himself a glorious Church.

The children of Israel could not enter into the Promised Land because of unbelief. Is it possible that those Christians who are denying that there

will be a Rapture will not be raptured themselves?

Several scriptures place strong emphasis on staying ready for the Rapture. After all, the event of Jesus' appearing is the *blessed* hope of the Church.

In Hebrews 9:28 Paul states: *Unto them that look for him shall he appear the second time.* Titus 2:13 says that we should be *looking for that blessed hope, and the glorious appearing of the great God and our Saviour Jesus Christ.* The people referred to in the above two verses are the same ones instructed by Jesus to *watch* and *pray* to enable them to escape all the events of the future and to stand with Him. (Luke 21:36.)

The word *look*, chosen by Paul (Heb. 9:28), and the word *watch*, chosen by Jesus (Luke 21:36), have the same basic meaning. The word *looking* in Titus 2:13 means ''to eagerly anticipate an event with preparation.'' All three words strongly imply ''commitment, dedication, alertness.''

A failure to watch, pray, and hopefully anticipate the appearing of Jesus places one in the category of the five foolish virgins (Matt. 25) or of the Laodicean lukewarm church (Rev. 3). Jesus made it very clear that those who are watching and praying *will be worthy* to escape.

Any Christian who does not believe in the Rapture is certainly not going to anticipate it or make any preparation. Paul and Titus collaborate to establish that believers must be actively anticipating the appearing of Jesus. I see the possibility of some born-again believers missing the Rapture, but with the present-day outpouring of the Holy Spirit, the probability is not so great. Not many believers will be ''lukewarm'' because they are getting fired up.

How did you determine that the one week referred to in Daniel 9:27 is actually seven years long?

The answer to this question is found in Daniel 9:24-27.

Daniel specifically speaks of a seventy-week period in which God is determined to perform six things in behalf of Israel. That period of time begins when Cyrus of Persia issues the decree for the rebuilding of the city of Jerusalem and the temple. The first seven weeks are used to rebuild Jerusalem and the second temple. Therefore, we discover quickly that these are weeks of years rather than weeks of days.

The first sixty-nine weeks see the rebuilding of the city and its temple, also the births and growing years of John the Baptist and Jesus. Daniel tells us that these sixty-nine weeks end with the crucifixion of Jesus. So the seventieth and final week will also be a week of years, not a week of days.

How many raptures are there in the Bible?

There are seven. Those people raptured are:

1. *Enoch*
   (Gen. 5:24; Heb. 11:5)

2. *Elijah*
   (2 Kings 2:11)

3. *Jesus*
   (Acts 1:9)

4. *The Church*
   (John 14:3; Luke 21:36; 1 Thess. 4:16,17; Heb. 9:28; Titus 2:13; Rev. 4:1,2)

5. *The Great Multitude at Mid-Tribulation*
   (Rev. 7:9-17)

6. *The 144,000 Jewish Evangelists*
   (Rev. 14:1-5)

7. *The Two Witnesses*
   (Rev. 11:3-12)

What Scripture verses support mid-Tribulation and post-Tribulation raptures?

Without a doubt, Revelation 7:9-17 sets the stage for a mid-Tribulation rapture. Notice that several things about this rapture are different from the catching up of the Church. There is no accompanying resurrection, nor does Jesus meet these believers in the air. All are taken up alive, and they do not sing the new song, as sung by the Church company. (Rev. 5:9.)

The Great Multitude, the people involved in this rapture, are the converts of the 144,000 who are taken up to escape the Antichrist's wrath when he breaks his agreement with Israel at mid-Tribulation.

Some teachers erroneously try to place the Rapture of the Church on the final day of the Tribulation. This is totally out of harmony with what the Bible teaches. The rapture taking place on that day consists of only two men—the Two Witnesses who are resurrected, then raptured. (Rev. 11:3-12.)

First Corinthians 15:23 states: *Every man in his own order: Christ the firstfruits; afterward they that are Christ's at his coming.* This scripture indicates that there will be multiple raptures, according to order and to separation by time.

Jesus is the firstfruits of a series of marvelous events. This verse also speaks of the gathering together of the Church. The Church is the first group to be caught up after Jesus, followed by the Great Multitude raptured at mid-Tribulation. The 144,000 Jewish evangelists are caught up about six months later. The last rapture is that of the Two Witnesses on the final day of the Tribulation. Excluding Jesus, this totals four raptures ordered by God between the closing of the church age and the end of the Tribulation Period.

Who are the Two Witnesses discussed in Revelation 11:3-13?

Because the Bible does not specifically name the Two Witnesses, we can only speculate as to their identities. The names usually submitted are: Enoch, Moses, Elijah, Joshua, Zerubbabel, and the Apostle John. I personally do not believe it is any of these six. The arguments used to support these selections are invalid.

Elijah and John are selected on the basis of verses from Malachi 4 and Revelation 10 which are as follows:

Behold, I will send you Elijah the prophet before the coming of the great and dreadful day of the Lord:

And he shall turn the heart of the fathers to the children, and the heart of the children to their fathers, lest I come and smite the earth with a curse.

Malachi 4:5,6

Thou must prophesy again before many peoples, and nations, and tongues, and kings.

Revelation 10:11

Elijah is also selected as a possibility on the basis of Hebrews 9:27 which states: *It is appointed unto men once to die.* Elijah was taken to heaven without tasting death (as was Enoch). However, I fail to see how this verse affirms his (or Enoch's) nomination. Because of Jesus' appearing, many of us will not see death.

Revelation 11 states that the Two Witnesses die and are resurrected. (vv. 7,11,12.) This eliminates John (as well as Moses, Joshua, and Zerubbabel) because he died and, as we saw above, man can die only once.

My conclusion is that if the sovereign God can choose 144,000 Jewish men to evangelize the world (Rev. 7:1-8), He can raise up two men out of the Tribulation Period to be the Two Witnesses. We will just have to wait and see.

What is the difference between "the trumpets" of 1 Corinthians 15:51,52, 1 Thessalonians 4:16, Matthew 24:31, and Revelation 11:15?

Let's examine these four passages of Scripture.

*Behold, I shew you a mystery; We shall not all sleep, but we shall all be changed, in a moment, in the twinkling of an eye, at **the last trump:** for the trumpet shall sound, and the dead shall be raised incorruptible, and we shall be changed.*

1 Corinthians 15:51,52

*For the Lord himself shall descend from heaven with a shout, with the voice of the archangel, and with **the trump** of God: and the dead in Christ shall rise first:*

Then we which are alive and remain shall be caught up together with them in the clouds, to meet the Lord in the air: and so shall we ever be with the Lord.

1 Thessalonians 4:16,17

*He (Jesus) shall send his angels with a great sound of **a trumpet,** and they shall gather together his elect from the four winds, from one end of heaven to the other.*

Matthew 24:31

*The **seventh angel sounded;** and there were great voices in heaven, saying, The*

28

kingdoms of this world are become the kingdoms of our Lord, and of his Christ; and he shall reign for ever and ever.

Revelation 11:15

The trumpet which Paul declared to be *the last trump* in 1 Corinthians 15 is the final signal from God for the Church to depart the earth and meet Christ in the air before proceeding to the throne of God.

This trumpet is the same as *the trump of God* in 1 Thessalonians 4. The event described in the passages surrounding each of the two scriptures is the same. Also you must keep in mind that Paul was writing to the Church about the plan of God affecting it, not about the Tribulation Period.

This trumpet is different from the great trumpet of Matthew 24. That one is the same as the last trumpet of Revelation 11, the seventh and final angelic trumpet which sounds on the final day of the Tribulation. It signals the end of that seven-year period with the return of Christ and His saints from heaven.

By no stretch of the imagination can the event which takes place with the sounding of the last trumpet of God (in 1 Cor. 15 and 1 Thess. 4) be the same set of circumstances which takes place with the sounding of the seventh angelic trumpet (in Rev. 11 and Matt. 24).

Let no one confuse you with the teaching that those two trumpets are the same!

If they were, the Church would not be caught up until the final day of the Tribulation. It would meet Christ in the air, do a U turn, and return immediately to earth, never going to heaven.

Such action would also contradict Jesus' statement: *Watch ye therefore, and pray always, that ye may be accounted worthy to escape all these things that shall come to pass, and to stand before the Son of man* (Luke 21:36).

Jesus said the followers referred to in the above verse would *escape* all the things of the future. Realize that were the Church not taken up until the last day of the Tribulation, it would escape the 1000-year reign of Christ.

The above discussion makes clear how unsound the teaching is which declares that the Church must go through the Tribulation before being caught up. Always remember that the Church must first arrive in heaven, then later reign with Jesus on earth.

What are those people who die in the Lord prior to the Rapture to anticipate? Where do their souls and spirits go? Do they go to the New Jerusalem in heaven?

The Apostle Paul tells us that to be absent from the body is to be with the Lord. (2 Cor. 5:8.) At a believer's death, his spirit and soul go immediately to be with the Lord in heaven. Therefore, to die prior to the Rapture is to experience victory over death. Remember, death has lost its sting for the believer. (1 Cor. 15:55.)

The dead in Christ are in paradise. This is not the same as the New Jerusalem.

According to 1 Thessalonians 4:16,17, *the dead in Christ shall rise first* in the Rapture. How can they if they are already in heaven?

The whole man is spirit, soul, and body. The spirits and souls of the dead in Christ are in heaven; the bodies in a burial place. Jesus died for the whole man. With the crucifixion of Christ, the great price was paid, and God purchased the whole man. Therefore, when Jesus appears, the body will be reunited with spirit and soul.

When Christ comes for that event, the saints in heaven—their spirits and souls—will come with Him. (v. 14.) This is the reason they have a brief advantage over the living Christians.

They will have enough time to be reunited with their resurrected bodies before we join them in the air.

Matthew 24:14 states: *And this gospel of the kingdom shall be preached in all the world for a witness unto all nations; and then shall the end come.* **Must the Word be preached to every nation or person before Jesus' Second Coming?**

The key to understanding the above verse is in examining the word *end*.

Before the Tribulation, the Church will preach the Gospel. During the first four years of the Tribulation, the 144,000 will carry the Gospel to the whole earth. From the midpoint to the end of the Tribulation, the angels will preach it. As nations will be saved during the 1000-year reign of Christ (Rev. 21:24), we know that the Gospel will still be preached during that period. Therefore, *the end* would have to be the end of all things which includes the reign of Christ on earth.

As long as it is here, the Church is responsible for preaching the Gospel. But we can see from the Scriptures that others are to be saved later on. So God will continue working on earth after the Church has been caught up.

Have all prophecies been fulfilled which would prevent the Lord's coming for the Church?

No, they have not. However, the rapidity with which prophecy is not being fulfilled is bringing us closer to that event.

The number one prophecy yet to be fulfilled has to do with the Church itself. It comes as the answer to Jesus' prayer, recorded in John 17:21: "Father, let them be one even as we are one that the world may know that You have sent me." This places responsibility upon the Church—all born-again followers of Jesus—to come together in the love of God. We are to be motivated by the Holy Spirit to lift up Jesus so that the whole world might come to know Him as their Savior.

Paul gives another prophetic aspect of the Church that needs to be fulfilled: maturity. (See 1 Cor. 12:12-14; Eph. 4:11-16.)

Could the explanation of the Feast of the Tabernacles (Lev. 23:42,43; Neh. 8:14-18) be an Old Testament shadow of the Rapture of the Church—its seven years of joy and its return at the beginning of the Millennium with Jesus? Are the accounts concerning Noah and Lot also Old Testament pictures of the Rapture?

Bible scholars have always recognized that within the Bible there are many "types and shadows" of things to come. We cannot build doctrine on types and shadows. However, they certainly do give us insight and additional understanding of Bible truths. Since the Old Testament record serves for our benefit as a foundation for the New Testament, I do see the shadow described in the question.

During the Feast of the Tabernacles, the Jews left their dwelling places to live in booths for seven days before returning. The activities of those seven days—feasting, merriment, partaking of the Word—were done as a witness to upcoming generations that the children of Israel were made to dwell in booths after God had delivered them from Egypt. On the eighth day there was a solemn assembly.

This is a shadow. The Church will be raptured, taken out of the world to spend seven joyful years of feasting (the Marriage Supper) and fellowship in a special place with the Lord. Then it will gloriously return with Him to establish His 1000-year reign on earth.

Of course, Noah and his family escaped the entire Flood; Lot and his family had to be completely away from Sodom before God released His wrath.

Both of these are excellent examples of the Rapture.

Explain the rebuilding of the temple.

This is an interesting subject to Christians because some people teach that the Rapture of the Church will not take place until the temple is rebuilt in Jerusalem. No chapter and verse in the Bible supports such teaching.

The prophet Zechariah clearly states that there will not be any rebuilding on the temple site in Jerusalem until it can be supervised by the "Branch." (Zech. 6:12.) The Branch is an Old Testament term identifying the Messiah. So until the Messiah Himself can supervise it, there will be no rebuilding of the temple. That places the time of the rebuilding early in the Millennium. However, a central house of worship has to be built in Jerusalem to satisfy the religious needs of the nation of Israel and the office needs of the Antichrist. At midpoint of the Tribulation Period, the

Antichrist invades Israel and sets up his world offices. (2 Thess. 2:4.)

This new synagogue is under construction right now. It is located in the heart of downtown Jerusalem on King George Street, next door to the International Rabbinical Headquarters and across from the Jerusalem Plaza Hotel. It should be completed in the near future.

Do the people who miss the Rapture and those who receive Christ during the Tribulation have to be killed to enter the Kingdom?

The answer is an emphatic *No!*

It is true that some who are saved during the Tribulation will be martyred. (Rev. 6:9-11.) But if all were martyred, no one would be alive to be caught up at mid-Tribulation. Martyrdom does not constitute salvation!

Will the children of unbelievers be taken in the Rapture?

I cannot find a specific answer to this question in the Scriptures. However, you must remember that we are not living under the Law, but under God's love. Children, I believe, are innocent until becoming old enough to be accountable for their sins. The age of accountability must vary with the child and his environment.

Since we are living in the era of God's grace, of His loving kindness, I personally feel that the children of unsaved parents will be taken in the Rapture with the believers. If this is true, though, it will create a greater dilemma for the parents and grandparents left behind.

The Apostle Paul gives us insight into what will happen to the children of saved parents. He tells us that if either parent is sanctified, set apart unto God, then the children are holy. (1 Cor. 7:14.) You must give your small children every advantage in knowing God and His plan of salvation. Unsaved parents could place their tiny children at a great disadvantage.

What should we be doing now to prepare ourselves and others for the appearing of the Lord?

Simply follow the Lord daily, deny yourself, and maintain love toward one another. Work with other believers for the propagation of the Gospel of Jesus Christ in whatever way you can. Lift up Jesus, win souls, grow spiritually. When you are involved with Jesus and the believing crowd, you won't worry about whether or not you are going to be ready.

Should we still pursue long-range plans Jesus has instilled in us, even though He is coming so soon?

The answer is, *Yes.*

Jesus said, *Occupy till I come* (Luke 19:13). We can view the word *occupy* in two different ways. In one sense *occupy* means ''to take possession of''; in the other, "to do business, to keep on doing business."

As the Holy Spirit is leading you, and some of the plans involve the future, don't change or attempt to change the leadership of the Holy Spirit. Go right on and do what you believe the Holy Spirit is directing you to do—God will bless it. You might be surprised: It may not take as long for Jesus to come as you think.

Considering that Jesus is coming soon, should a person attending high school or college date and / or marry?

A young person should go right ahead getting his education and expecting his life to be fully developed. Although we know that the time of Jesus' appearing is getting close, we do not know the day nor the hour. (Mark 13:32.) The Scriptures instruct us to go right on enjoying the life that God has given us and preparing to enjoy it all the more while we serve Him and look for Jesus' return. (Luke 19:13.)

Do you have to be filled with the Holy Ghost with the evidence of speaking in tongues to go in the Rapture?

The answer is, *No.* The Bible does not teach this. Until the day the trumpet of God sounds, the Church will be working at its assignment, getting folks into the Kingdom. The Church will have just won thousands of people who won't even know that there is a Holy Ghost. Would those people be left behind? Of course not. Our God is not that kind of God.

What happens to people who are saved after the fifth year of the Tribulation, after the Wedding Feast?

They will remain on earth, awaiting Jesus Who will return to begin His 1000-year Kingdom.

Will people receive the Holy Ghost during the Tribulation?

I know of no scripture that establishes whether or not people will receive the Holy Ghost and speak in tongues during the Tribulation. However, we know the Holy Spirit will be at work on earth. Multitudes will be saved which, of course, is the work of the Holy Spirit.

I believe God's plan, as we know it, will continue. If we need the Holy Spirit today as Guide, Teacher, and Comforter, He would certainly be a vital companion for anyone saved during the so-called Tribulation Period.

Will the Tribulation Period be more severe in some parts of the world than in others? Will whether a nation has blessed or opposed Israel have any bearing on the severity of the Tribulation in that country?

A study of The Revelation reveals that even though the Tribulation is awesome, it will not be worldwide. Of course, the nations that have blessed and assisted Israel will be less affected than others because they will come under God's blessing of Genesis 12:3. On the basis of the same Scripture verse, the nations that have opposed Israel will come under God's curse.

The Tribulation will be confined to an area, affecting primarily the European-Mediterranean countries. A study of the book of Revelation reveals that the plagues and wrath of God are more concentrated upon the areas controlled by the Antichrist.

Where do the four horsemen of the Apocalypse fit into the Tribulation?

The four horsemen, described in Revelation 6, will be responsible for the death of one fourth of the earth's population over the seven-year Tribulation Period. (v. 8.)

Will Israel start animal sacrifices again?

It is rumored that some small sacrifices have already been offered within the Orthodox Jewish community. I don't know whether or not this is true.

Although Israel is about to have a central house of worship, the Great Synagogue, I do not foresee a renewal of animal sacrifices before the early part of the Tribulation.

Will Israel be under the Mosaic covenant during the Tribulation?

During the Tribulation, most of Israel will be saved and, therefore, will be redeemed from the curse of the Law. However, until the people of Israel are saved, they will be under Mosaic law.

Who will survive the Tribulation and live during the Millennium?

Even though the wrath of both God and Satan are poured out during the seven-year Tribulation, the Scriptures establish clearly that people from all over the earth will survive. These are:

A remnant of Israelis (Rev. 12:14)

The Arabs (Is. 19:23-25; Zech. 14:18,19)

People of all nations which came against Jerusalem (Zech. 14:16)

According to Revelation 21:24, many nations will be saved during the 1000-year reign of Christ.

Anyone who survives the Tribulation will have to refuse the mark of the Beast and the worship of his image.

What will everyday life be like for people living during the Millennium?

Although the Bible does not give us detailed insight into what everyday life will be like during the Millennium, it does establish that the peace and righteousness of God will abound during those 1000 years.

Jesus will personally rule all nations. The Church company will be His administrators as kings and priests. There will be no wars, nor will implements of war exist. Animals will be tame—the lion will lay down with the lamb; the wolf and the calf will eat side by side. Children playing outside will encounter nothing that can harm them. (Is. 11:5-9.)

We can't speculate beyond what insight the Scriptures give us, but let's conclude that life will be much better than it is even at its best today!

Will only Christians be living on earth during the Millennium?

The answer is, *No!*

Revelation 21:24 teaches that during the Millennium there will be salvation of nations. Revelation 20 teaches that when Satan is released from the bottomless pit at the end of the Millennium, there are unsaved who will follow him.

Consider these two passages of Scripture: Revelation 2:27 and 19:15. They tell us that both Jesus and the overcomers (the Church) will rule with the rod of iron, which means firm authority. If only the righteous occupied the earth, why would there be any need for "firm authority"?

Who occupies the earth during the Millennium?

1. *The saints from heaven* (Zech. 14:5; Rev. 17:14)

2. *The remnant of Israel which had been hidden away for three and one-half years* (Rev. 12:13-17)

3. *The resurrected martyrs* (Rev. 6:9-11; 11:11,12)

4. *The unsaved survivors of that period* (Is. 19:23-25; Zech. 14:16; Rev. 21:24)

Isn't God's plan fabulous?

What events take place after the Millennium?

Revelation 20, 21, and 22 give us the answer. The scenario runs like this:

Satan is released from the bottomless pit for only a short time. He goes about getting an earthly following from the people born during the Millennium who had chosen not to accept Christ. God destroys this company and casts Satan into the lake of fire forever.

The final resurrection occurs. All the wicked are turned into the place of everlasting punishment, and the righteous inherit the new earth and the New Jerusalem.

Why is Satan released from the bottomless pit at the end of the Millennium? Who are the people who then join him and revolt against God?

Satan is released for a short season (Rev. 20:7) to allow men the right to exercise their free moral agency. God is just!

During the Millennium, no one has any choice but to worship Jesus. Many people accept Him and fall in love with Him, while others only do Him lip service. God releases Satan so that those who wish to follow him may do so. The people who join Satan come from among the nations on the earth, not from among the redeemed.

How will it be when we return after the 1000-year reign of Christ? Will we live as we have before? What will our bodies be like? Will we be married and live with our families?

When Jesus appears to receive the glorious Church unto Himself, the bodies of those caught up will immediately be glorified. . . . *when he shall appear, we shall be like him* (1 John 3:2). We will be *completely* like Jesus!

Examine these two Scripture verses:

Ought not Christ to have suffered these things, and to enter into his glory? (Luke 24:26).

Jesus saith unto her, Mary . . . touch me not; for I am not yet ascended to my Father (John 20:16,17).

From these we learn that Jesus was to be glorified and that Mary could not touch Him until He had ascended to the Father.

Hebrews 2:14 states: *Forasmuch then as the children are partakers of flesh and blood, he also himself likewise took part of the same.*

The above three scriptures cause me to believe that, like everyone else, Jesus was indeed flesh and blood. Upon His resurrection it was necessary for Him to be *totally* glorified, His body included.

Following His resurrection, His glorified body was so perfect that He was able to pass through a solid mass. In a closed room He simply appeared, in bodily form, before His disciples in Jerusalem. (Luke 24:36.) However, we can see that Jesus still had a very real body. When He appeared to the disciples, He said, *Behold my hands and my feet, that it is I myself: handle me, and see; for a spirit hath not flesh and bones, as ye see me have* (v. 39).

He also had an appetite for real food. In verse 41 Jesus asked, *Have ye here any meat?* Verses 42 and 43 state: *They gave him a piece of a broiled fish, and of an honeycomb. And he took it, and did eat before them.*

From the above Scripture verses, we can be sure that we, too, will have real bodies, glorified bodies—just like Jesus' body was!

God has not chosen to give us full insight into our future. We don't know whether there will be differentiation between male and female. God has told us, though, that we will be like the angels and not have reproductive ability.

The children of this world marry, and are given in marriage: but they which shall be accounted worthy to obtain that world, and the resurrection from the dead, neither marry, nor are given in marriage:

Neither can they die any more: for they are equal unto the angels; and are the children of God, being the children of the resurrection.

Luke 20:34-36

God also tells us that we shall be known as we were known. (1 Cor. 13:12.)

As to whether or not we will still live as husbands, wives, and families, we will have to wait and see. This we know: Our relationship then will be on a higher plane and in a dimension greater than our present one.

Who occupies the new earth after the Millennium?

1. *The Church*
   (Rev. 21 and 22)

2. *The Tribulation saints*
   (Rev. 7:9-17)

3. *The natural people saved during the Millennium, descendants of the Arabs referred to in Zechariah 14:16*
   (Rev. 21:24)

4. *The natural people of Israel, the hidden remnant who were saved but remained mortal*
   (Rev. 12:13-17)

Who is "the elect" of Matthew 24?

This answer requires a brief Bible study.

The Gospel of Matthew was written for the Jews; Mark for the Romans; Luke for the Greeks; and John for the Church, the New Testament believers.

Let's examine some references to "the elect."

Except those days (of the Tribulation) *should be shortened, there should no flesh be saved: but for the elect's sake those days shall be shortened.*

Matthew 24:22

Then (after the Tribulation) *shall they see the Son of man coming in the clouds with great power and glory.*

And then shall he send his angels, and shall gather together his elect from the four winds, from the uttermost part of the earth to the uttermost part of heaven.

Mark 13:26,27

The elect of Matthew 24 refers to the Jews; but after examining the elect in the above passages, you will discover that the total company of the elect is present with Jesus upon His return to earth.

Consider that there are four distinct "elects" of God in the Scriptures:

1. *Israel*
   (Is. 42:1; 45:4; 65:9; Matt. 24:22)

2. *The Church*
   (Rom. 8:33; Col. 3:12; 2 Tim. 2:10; Titus 1:1; 1 Pet. 1:2; 5:13)

3. *Angels*
   (1 Tim. 5:21)

4. *Jesus*
   (1 Pet. 2:6)

At Jesus' return the elect, including the angels, are gathered to Him from heaven and earth—all four at once.

What are the rewards, the crowns of the saints?

Jesus teaches that we shall be rewarded according to our works.

The Bible does not spell out all the rewards, but among those listed are: life everlasting, the privilege of being with Jesus and with our heavenly Father, a heavenly dwelling place, the New Jerusalem, a gold crown, a throne, and an abundance of all the things over which we have been faithful on the earth.

What is the *mystery of iniquity* of 2 Thessalonians 2:7?

The term *mystery of iniquity* means "unexplained wickedness." It refers to a plan designed to bring forth Satan's likeness in the flesh just as Jesus was God Who came in the flesh.

Paul teaches that the presence of the anointed and powerful Church has caused Satan to withhold continually his insidious plan. (Remember, the "*he* that must be taken out of the way" is the Church.)

Now ye know what withholdeth that he might be revealed in his time.

For the mystery of iniquity doth already work: only he who now letteth will let, until he be taken out of the way (vv. 6,7).

Notice that Paul states the mystery of iniquity was already at work in his day. This information reveals how long Satan has been unsuccessfully attempting to activate his plan. The spirit of lawlessness, or of the Antichrist, has been evident throughout the church age; but there will be no actual manifestation of the Antichrist until the Church has been caught up.

What are the spots and blemishes referred to in Ephesians 5:27?

The Scripture verse in question states:

That he (Jesus) *might present it to himself a glorious church, not having spot, or wrinkle, or any such thing; but that it should be holy and without blemish.*

Second Peter 2:9-19 describes at length certain kinds of people in the

Church who focus attention on themselves by declaring how spiritual they are. They always attempt to gain a small following by deceiving new Christians, who have little or no foundation in the Word.

The Scriptures speak strongly against such persons and clearly establish that the Church will be cleansed of such kind.

Who are the twenty-four elders in Revelation 4 and 5?

The twenty-four elders are described as sitting on thrones, wearing white raiment (robes of righteousness), and wearing crowns. (See Rev. 4:4 AMP.) They sing the new song of the redeemed in which they confess, ''We represent all races and nations of people and all languages on the earth. We have been redeemed by the blood of the Lamb, and we shall reign as kings and priests on the earth.'' (Rev. 5:9.) This description is that of every born-again follower of Jesus Christ according to the New Testament.

By the number *twenty-four*, we know that they are representatives. This is the double twelve of God's Word: twelve representing the twelve tribes of Israel, and twelve representing the twelve apostles of the Lamb from the church age.

Throughout the New Testament, the word *elder* identifies one who is called to represent the Church of the Lord Jesus Christ on the earth. Because all the single representatives of the Church are in heaven and because all the angels are present around the throne, we know that the entire Church is in heaven. If it weren't, the angels wouldn't be there. Angels are on divine assignment on behalf of the Church. (Heb. 1:13,14.) The twenty-four elders are selected representatives of the Church company in heaven.

Who is the Bride of Christ?

The following Scripture passage reveals the truth:

And there came unto me one of the seven angels which had the seven vials full of the seven last plagues, and talked with me, saying, Come hither, I will shew thee the bride, the Lamb's wife.

And he carried me away in the spirit to a great and high mountain, and shewed me that great city, the holy Jerusalem, descending out of heaven from God.

Revelation 21:9,10

We can see from this that the Lamb's bride is made up of the New Jerusalem. The Church is the Body of Christ of which Christ is the Head. Since the Church is His Body, He and the Church will occupy the New Jerusalem, which is adorned as a bride.

Are the people saved during the Tribulation part of the Bride of Christ?

I find nothing in the book of Revelation that supports this idea. I believe they would have to be of the Body of Christ, like all other believers.

If the Bride of Christ is the city New Jerusalem and the Body is the Church, who are the guests at the Marriage Supper of the Lamb spoken of in Revelation 19:9?

The guests are the Great Multitude caught up at mid-Tribulation. (See Rev. 7:9-17.) They would also be part of His Body but not of the Church company. Only the 144,000 (Rev. 14:1-5) are permitted to join the Church company.

Who or what are the seven Spirits before the throne of God as mentioned in Revelation 1:4 and 4:5?

The seven Spirits are symbolic of the Holy Spirit. There is only one Holy Spirit, but He has many diversities, offices, and administrations.

If you want to learn more about this, I recommend that you study Isaiah 11, 1 Corinthians 12, Ephesians 4, and other scriptures.

Who is the red dragon in Revelation 12?

The red dragon is identified clearly throughout Revelation as Satan. (See especially v. 9.)

Who is the woman of Revelation 12 who gives birth to a man-child?

The woman is Israel. Giving her any other identity would be unharmonious with the biblical story. Notice that the Antichrist goes to make war with her seed and Satan attempts to devour the baby.

Who is the child in Revelation 12:2-5?

Since the woman in this chapter is Israel, the child can only be Jesus.

Note: The child cannot be the Bride nor the 144,000 as some erroneously teach. Revelation 21:9,10 establishes the Bride as the city New Jerusalem. The 144,000 are sealed, which makes them immune from all harm. (Rev. 7:4; 14:1.)

Who are the martyrs of Revelation 6:9-11?

John saw these martyred ones when the fifth seal was opened. They are members of the Great Multitude who are saved during the Tribulation, but are slain for the testimony of Jesus. (Rev. 6:9.)

What are the demon locusts of Revelation 9?

These are insects described as having the scorpion's sting. Rather than feeding on vegetation, they torment the people who are without the seal of God on their foreheads.

Many people have attempted to interpret these locusts as jet aircraft. I strongly disagree with this idea.

All Scripture must be interpreted literally. The only exception to this occurs when the context of the Scripture clearly establishes that a figure of speech or a symbol is being used. In this case, I believe the insects are literally locusts.

Who are those mentioned in Revelation 20:4,5?

This Scripture passage says:

And I (John) saw thrones, and they sat upon them, and judgment was given unto them: and I saw the souls of them that were beheaded for the witness of Jesus, and for the word of God, and which had not worshipped the beast, neither his image, neither had received his mark upon their foreheads, or in their hands; and they lived and reigned with Christ a thousand years.

But the rest of the dead lived not again until the thousand years were finished. This is the first resurrection.

Those seen upon thrones to whom judgment was given are the Church saints who had returned to earth with Christ.

The souls of the beheaded are the resurrected martyrs of the Tribulation.

The rest of the dead not to be resurrected until the end of the Millennium are the wicked dead of all time.

Who is the great whore of Revelation 17:1-10?

The great whore (also referred to as the Harlot) is the personification of false religion. It is an amalgamation of all man's religions into one organization such as the World Council of Churches.

The Harlot has always controlled masses of people; thus, she is important to the Antichrist. Such a system has existed since the early Babylonian Empire.

Some people say that the United States, not the harlot religious system, is the national Babylon of Revelation 18. They base this idea on Revelation 18:10-19, interpreting it to suggest that the United States coastal cities will come under atomic attack. Does this interpretation have any basis?

This teaching, prevalent for years, isn't true. The Babylonian system and the Harlot date back to the Babylonian Empire. Furthermore, this identification is usually made by those who see nothing good or godly about the United States.

In actuality, the U.S. is the most blessed nation in the world. As the major backer of Israel and as the peace-maker, she is blessed. (Gen. 12:3; Matt. 5:9.) Besides having these two great assignments, the U.S. is God's arm of evangelism in carrying out the Great Commission: *Go ye into all the world, and preach the gospel to every creature.*

Don't accept the same negative attitude toward the United States as Jonah had toward Ninevah. Jonah was so caught up by the wickedness of Ninevah that he believed they deserved to have the wrath of God poured upon them. In other words, Jonah took it on himself to judge Ninevah, just as some judge the U.S.A. Remember, God is

Judge and we must work as an evangelist. No one should attempt to pronounce God's wrath.

What empires are represented by the different materials composing the statue in Nebuchadnezzar's dream from Daniel 2:32-35?

From Daniel's interpretation (vv. 38-46), we know that the golden head represents the Babylonian Empire, while the silver chest and arms symbolize the Persian Empire. The belly and thighs of brass identify the Greek Empire under Alexander the Great. The legs of iron and the feet of iron and clay clearly identifies the Roman Empire.

Is the Common Market of Europe a restoration of the old Roman Empire described in Nebuchadnezzar's dream?

The European Common Market is not a restoration of the Roman Empire. It is the seventh head of the evil Beast System which produced not only the

Roman, but all the empires: Egyptian, Assyrian, Babylonian, Persian, and Greek.

What is the seven-headed, ten-horned Beast?

The seven-headed Beast identifies a satanic system of empires. (Rev. 13:1-3.) John tells us in Revelation 17 that five of those heads or empires had already fallen and that one existed at the time he was receiving the prophecy.

The five which had fallen were the heads of the Egyptian, Assyrian, Babylonian, Persian, and Greek empires. The empire that existed in John's day—the sixth head of the Beast—was the Roman Empire.

The seventh head will result from the coming together of ten horns. These ten horns are the European nations of the Common Market which, when Greece took membership on January 1, 1981, became a ten-nation federation.

Out of this seventh head will come the eighth—the Antichrist.

The Beast System will have two leaders. Both men—the Antichrist (Rev. 13:5-8) and the False Prophet (Rev. 13:11-16)—are also called the Beast.

Revelation 13:7 says that the Beast will be given power to conquer the saints still on the earth. This seems inconsistent with God's character. Does God give him this power?

According to verse 2 of the same chapter, the dragon (Satan) gives the Antichrist his assignment, not God. It is Satan who would like for someone to overcome the saints for him since he cannot. However, because the Church will have already been caught up, Satan's plan is totally frustrated.

The Antichrist gains control over thirteen European and Mediterranean nations, three of which he destroys. His success is limited and brief.

Why is one Antichrist emphasized so strongly when the Scriptures speak of many antichrists existing throughout the church age?

Jesus often speaks of the "false" ones and John clearly establishes the existence of many antichrists. (1 John 2:18,19,22; 4:3.)

From these same references John speaks of the one Antichrist which shall come. He, the Antichrist, is also called the "man of sin," the "son of perdition," and the "wicked one" by Paul. (2 Thess. 2:3,8,9.)

Keep in mind, also, that a condition which differentiates a single Antichrist is that he cannot be revealed until the Church has been caught up. (2 Thess. 2:7,8.)

Does the Antichrist come out of the Church as the Scriptures reveal?

First John 2:18,19 refers to the *many antichrists* who *went out from us, but . . .*

were not of us. As discussed above, these people are not the same as the Antichrist, the ''wicked one.''

Do the Scriptures indicate that the Antichrist might be a Jew?

Many believe that the Antichrist will have to be a Jew because the Israelis could not accept him as the Messiah if he were not a Jew. Certainly they couldn't. But Israel is not going to accept him as the Messiah. No chapter and verse in the Bible supports this idea.

The Antichrist does gain a treaty with Israel. Why? Because Israel will have just destroyed the giant Russia in one day with God's help, and the Antichrist will want her favor. He enters into a seven-year treaty with her. (Dan. 9:24-27.)

Because of a statement concerning the Antichrist in Daniel 11:37 that he shall not regard the God of his fathers, some people have assumed that he would have to be Jewish. However, there is no reason why he could not be an apostate reprobate Gentile.

Will the Antichrist be mortally wounded, then resurrected by the False Prophet?

First, upon carefully studying Revelation 17, you will discover that it is the sixth head of the Beast System which is wounded mortally, not the Antichrist. The sixth head was the Roman Empire, including the Egyptian, Assyrian, Babylonian, Persian, and Greek empires—the first five heads. Number six, the Roman Empire, was struck a mortal blow by Jesus, the stone of Daniel 2:34,35,44.

Second, remember that the False Prophet does not have resurrection power. Only God the Holy Spirit has resurrection power. (Rom. 8:11.) However, he does help the Antichrist restore the System which produces the seventh and eighth heads. Later, both are destroyed totally when Jesus and the Church return from heaven.

Does the man who is going to be the Antichrist know beforehand what his role is going to be during the Tribulation Period?

The Scriptures do not reveal whether or not the person will know his assignment prior to the Tribulation. I believe Satan will enter him just as he did Judas. Judas was a type of the Antichrist.

What is the Illuminati? Will the Antichrist be linked to it?

The Illuminati is identified with mysticism and dates back several centuries. We know that in 1520 it was crushed by the Spanish Inquisition. Around 1623 it sprang up in France and was suppressed in 1635, only to reappear in 1722. The French Revolution then destroyed it.

Once more it sprang up in Belgium and Germany in the second half of the 18th century. The Roman Catholic Church condemned the movement. As a result of government decree, it was dissolved in 1785.

Then along came the Rosicrucian movement which also called itself the Illuminati.

The Illuminati claimed that they were able to receive spiritual illumination through the cultivation of an inner light. Consider what the Bible says: *Satan himself is transformed into an angel of light. Therefore it is no great thing if his ministers* (spiritualist mediums of all sorts) *also be transformed as the ministers of righteousness; whose end shall be according to their works* (2 Cor. 11:14,15).

The Antichrist will be a spiritualist medium of the highest order. (See Dan. 8:23-25; 2 Thess. 2:9.) This does not mean, however, that he will head the Illuminati.

I know of no present order of Illuminati, although there is an existing order of Rosicrucians based in San Diego, California. However, anyone who is controlled by any form of witchcraft, occultism, or Eastern religion believes in cultivating a so-called inner light, the basic belief of the Illuminati. The people who hold this idea are possessed by a familiar spirit.

Do not try to visualize this organization. Just consider all spiritualist mediums to be members and know that their total source is Satan. Remember that Satan is a champion loser! He has no power. Because he is a liar in whom there is no truth, his organizations never exist very long and he has to start over again. Just as Satan is a loser, so will the Antichrist be a loser!

Who is the False Prophet?

The personal identity of the False Prophet is as hidden as that of the Antichrist. His role will be that of convincing the people to take the mark of the Beast and to worship its image. (Rev. 13:11-17.)

From this information, we can see that this man definitely will be a renowned religious leader, one who has gained great influence with the organized church world. It is apparent that the Antichrist needs his assistance if he is to carry out successfully his evil assignment.

The organization which presently comes closest to fulfilling the Harlot's description of Revelation 17 is the World Council of Churches of Geneva, Switzerland. It is reasonable to consider that the man who will eventually head this organization is likely to be the False Prophet.

The False Prophet will possess the powers of witchcraft, as will the Antichrist, placing him in the category of a top spiritualist medium. Were the maturing Church to know the true identity of the False Prophet, it could work great spiritual bondage against him and render him ineffective. This is the major reason his true identity is cloaked.

What is 666, the mark of the Beast?

The mark of the Beast is discussed exclusively in Revelation 13:16-18. It is a mark of the System headed by the Antichrist, used to identify all people who worship and follow the Beast. Verse 18 declares it to be a triple six, which represents the unholy trinity.

This mark is to be borne either on the forehead or in the palm of the right hand.

There can be no salvation for those people who take the mark of the Beast. The moment they take it, they seal their eternal doom.

Will the mark of the Beast be used worldwide?

Satan intends for the mark to be used worldwide. However, since God does not allow Satan to run without restraint, the best Satan can do is gain control over nations in the European area with pockets of followers in other countries. At the height of his success, the Antichrist is able to bring only ten nations of the European-Mediterranean area under his control. He does not become a world dictator or president.

If everyone in the world took the mark, no one would survive the Tribulation. We know from Isaiah 19 and Zechariah 14 that the Arabs survive without taking the mark. Also, the remnant of Israel survives (Rev. 12:14), as well as survivors of all nations. (Zech. 14:16.) The mark of the Beast will not be used worldwide.

There have been reports of some people receiving Social Security checks stating, ''Not negotiable if number does not correspond with mark on forehead or hand.'' Apparently, when questioned, the Social Security office

stated that the checks were not supposed to be issued until 1982 or 1984. Is this the mark of the Beast?

No proof has been found of any existing Social Security checks requiring a matching number either on the bearer's forehead or right hand. My opinion about the rumor is that someone started the hoax knowing gullible Christians would run scared.

A study of 2 Thessalonians 2:1-9 reveals that the Antichrist and his program cannot begin while the Church is still on earth. Revelation 13:16-18 describes the mark which is introduced at mid-Tribulation.

Since the Tribulation cannot even begin until the Church has been taken up, no one should be concerned over this rumor. The implementation of the System using the mark referred to in Revelation is still years away.

Some predictions have declared the collapse of our money system. Are these statements prophetically sound?

No Scripture lends itself to the support of such predictions. A cashless society will not exist during the church age or even after. Such a system is in the process of being perfected by the world banking interest, but is not ready to be set in order.

The Word of God teaches us, as followers of God, to be good stewards of the tithe. God explained the meaning of the tithe when he said, ''A tenth of all is mine.'' (Lev. 27:30-33.)

God has ordained that His work be supported by His people through their tithes and offerings. God blesses His people who support His work through the tithe.

Bring ye all the tithes into the storehouse, that there may be meat in mine house, and prove me now herewith, saith the Lord of hosts, if I will not open you the windows of heaven, and pour you out a blessing, that there shall not be room enough to receive it.

Malachi 3:10

Satan would like to create a cashless society. If our money systems were to utterly fail and a new system be established that was completely controlled by the government, God's people would be destitute. They would be unable to tithe. This would cause God's work to shut down. Satan, working through the new system, would then cut off all flow of money to the Church. Evangelism, missions, and all other operations for God would cease.

But realize that the Devil has never been that successful, nor will he be. The plans being made for a cashless society will never be perfected. God's work will not shut down. This idea is contrary to what the Scriptures teach. Consider the following Bible truths:

81

The Church is the head and not the tail (Deut. 28:44); the light of the world and the salt of the earth (Matt. 5:13,14); and the representative of Jesus (Acts 1:8; John 13:34,35; 2 Cor. 3:3). Paul declares that the Church will increase. (Eph. 4:11-16.) The prophets Isaiah and Micah confirm the increase in the last days. (See Is. 2:2; Mic. 4:1.)

We are living in the last days now, and the Word of God tells us that the time preceding the sounding of God's trumpet is going to be a prosperous period.

Jesus said, ''As it was in the days of Noah before the Flood, and as it was in the days of Lot before the destruction of Sodom, so shall it also be in the day when the Son of Man is revealed.'' (Luke 17:26-30.)

For what reason is the Son of Man going to be revealed? The Apostle Paul states that Jesus will be revealed to receive the glorious Church unto Himself. (Eph. 5:27.) So from now until the sounding of the trumpet of God, prosperity will be the major condition of the world's economy.

Inflation will be increasing; but as we saw before, the Church has an assignment to carry out—an assignment involving increase. Therefore, the Church's money will also be increasing!

God said that He will teach us to get riches. *It is he that giveth thee power to get wealth* (Deut. 8:18). God causes gain (money and things) to come to us from other people. Jesus said, *Give, and it shall be given unto you; good measure, pressed down, and shaken together, and running over, shall men give into your bosom* (Luke 6:38).

Besides instructing the Church to be good stewards of its money through tithing, God also instructs it in how to be New Testament givers: to give *more* than the tithe. This also results in increase (as we saw in Luke 6:38).

Jesus said, *Seek ye first the kingdom of God, and his righteousness; and all these things shall be added unto you* (Matt. 6:33). (Don't confuse earthly gain with godliness; however, know that godliness will bring you earthly gain.) You can see by the authority of His Word that God has planned for believers to have money to give—always.

Those people who become followers of God through Jesus Christ and are obedient to the Word will be good stewards of that which belongs to God. Stop worrying that you are not going to have any money. A cashless society will never exist.

Is the description in Isaiah 2:4 concerned with the last days of the Millennium, especially the reference to the nations not at war?

And he shall judge among the nations, and shall rebuke many people: and they shall beat their swords into plowshares, and their spears into pruninghooks: nation shall not lift up sword against nation, neither shall they learn war any more.

Isaiah 2:4

This verse speaks clearly about the last days being the beginning of the Millennium. (See also Mic. 4:3.) However, the flowing of people of all nations into the Kingdom of God continues right into the Millennium.

The tremendous event of salvation begins through the Church and continues through the Tribulation Period by the ministry of the 144,000 and the angels. (Rev. 7:1-8; 14:1-5,6-10.) Entire nations will be saved during the Millennium. (Rev. 21:24.) Keep in mind that the last days include the Tribulation, but not the Millennium.

When did the last days begin?

The last days began with the outpouring of the Holy Spirit on the Jewish feast day of Pentecost. We know this because the event was prophesied by Joel. (Joel 2:28,29.) When the event actually occurred, the Apostle Peter explained it to the observing crowd and declared it to be the beginning of the last days. (Acts 2:16-21.) Notice that Joel did not speak of the last days, but Peter was permitted by the Holy Spirit to associate the Holy Spirit experience to the last days. So we have now had more that 1900 years of last days.

The last days covers the period of the life of Christ, the church age, and the seven years of Tribulation. *Last days, times of the Gentiles,* and *church age*—all are synonymous.

For the 2000 years mentioned by the prophet Hosea, when do we begin counting, at the day of Pentecost?

No. The 2000-year period established by Hosea (Hos. 6:1-3) begins with the coming of the Savior, the birth of Jesus.

The period must include the life and ministry of Jesus, the complete church age, and the seven years of God's master performance which includes Tribulation.

In Luke 21:25 Jesus mentions a time preceding His return when there will be *distress of nations, with perplexity.* Has this prophecy begun to be fulfilled?

After examining the words that Jesus chooses, we can see that the period has already begun. The word *perplexity* is the key. It means to be embarrassed over problems that the nations have great difficulty resolving.

All nations existing today are distressed with severe internal problems that they are wrestling with great difficulty to control. This fulfills Jesus' prophecy of Luke 21:25.

After describing events of the last days, Jesus made this statement: *This generation shall not pass away, till all be fulfilled* (Luke 21:32). What time frame is being covered?

Inevitably, teachers fall into the snare of trying to establish forty years as being a generation. Jesus clearly establishes that this time frame begins with the rebirth of Israel. That occurred on May 15, 1948. One has to keep in mind that Jesus said those witnessing this rebirth would see the fulfillment of *all* things.

The generation referred to will be the "extended generation" in order for all prophecy to be fulfilled. Therefore, this generation will experience the glorious conclusion of the church age, the seven years emphasized by Revelation, plus the 1000-year reign of Jesus on earth.

When will the "falling away" of 2 Thessalonians, chapter 2, take place?

Let's examine this portion of Scripture.

Now we beseech you, brethren, by the coming of our Lord Jesus Christ, and by our gathering together unto him . . . (v. 1). Paul is clearly talking about the Rapture of the Church—the time when Jesus will appear and the Church will be gathered together unto Him.

. . . *that ye be not soon shaken in mind, or be troubled, neither by spirit, nor by word, nor by letter as from us, as that the day of Christ is at hand* (v. 2). From this verse it is apparent that there were those who passed through Thessalonica and taught that Christ was already at hand and that the Second Coming of Christ had already been fulfilled. Paul is having to write that church and get them straightened out.

Paul goes on to say: *Let no man deceive you by any means: for that day . . .* (What day? The day of Christ being at hand, the day that Christ will literally return to begin His 1000-year reign.) *. . . that day shall not come, except there come a falling away first, and that man of sin be revealed, the son of perdition.* The ''son of perdition'' is the Antichrist. So before Jesus comes to reign, there must be a falling away and a time of the Antichrist's administration.

At this time, while some churches are running over with people, other churches are struggling to maintain good attendance. The "falling away" is in process right now. If that be the case, we must also be approaching the time for the release of the Antichrist.

A considerable number of Jewish believers have come to the Lord since 1967. How does this fit into prophecy?

In 1967, the city of Jerusalem was repossessed by the armies of Israel during the Six-Day War. When that event occurred, it brought the times of the Gentiles into fulfillment. (See Luke 21:24.)

Immediately, the Holy Spirit stepped up His operation to bring the Church to a glorious conclusion, so that it could be received by Jesus. This intensification of the Holy Spirit's work has pierced the veil of the Jews, though not removing it. Many young Jews who were not involved in Judaism caught a glimpse of the Messiah and accepted Him.

Will Christians suffer great persecution in these last days?

The answer to this question is dependent upon one's definition of *persecution*. Actually, Christians are already undergoing severe opposition.

In America, liberal congressmen and TV personalities have put together a number of committees to make the Christian a second-rate citizen with no right to participate in national affairs. Battles have recently been fought concerning Christian TV. In addition, the American Civil Liberties Union (ACLU) has become a definite adversary of the Church.

Such conditions in countries other than America would cause Christians to be extremely hard pressed. But in America, a Christian can lead a peaceable life, one which will allow him to concentrate on godliness, by obeying the Scriptures and praying for those in authority. (1 Tim. 2:1-4.)

I do not foresee the kind of persecution that the early Church encountered, but a persecution of a more subtle, sophisticated nature. Remember, the believers are the glorious Church of the end times. They will operate in more faith and knowledge than any previous generations.

The Church of the last days will have organized opposition, but will have far more godly power and influence than ever before.

Note: Persecution never has come to *cause* the Church to obey God; it has always come *because the Church was obeying* the Word of God!

What was the Jupiter Effect which occurred in early 1982?

The Jupiter Effect, so-called within the Church, refers to the 1982-alignment of the planets in the Milky Way galaxy.

According to the late scientist, Dr. Wernher Von Braun, approximately every 180 years the planets line up perfectly. When the planets are in their natural orbit, it would take a spaceship forty-one years to encircle and film them. When they are in their perfect alignment, they can be examined by a spaceship in nine short years.

The United States launched the first spaceships for this project in 1973; the last ones were launched in 1979. By late 1982, we will have filmed at close range every major planet in this galaxy. The present generation is the first to have the technology to perform such an amazing feat.

The prophetic significance of this event is very exciting. Daniel 12:4 says we will know the time of the end has come by man's high mobility and his ever-increasing knowledge. The present generation is the one of rapidly increasing knowledge that has moved it into the space age.

Because this has never happened before, we know we are not just in the last days, but in the closing out period of the last days. The achievement of using our space vehicles to examine the planets of this galaxy proves conclusively that the explosion of knowledge is allowing us to play in God's frontyard!

How do you explain your interpretation of an airborne attack on Israel when the Scriptures refer to *raiders on horseback?*

God reveals through the prophet Ezekiel the future attempt by Russia of the north to take over the new nation of Israel.* (Ezek. 38.)

This prophecy is totally dependent upon there being a state of Israel. At the time Ezekiel set forth this prophecy, all Israel was in captivity. In order for this

---

*We can identify the Magog of Ezekiel 38 and 39 as Russia. On old biblical maps, the territories and provinces described as being in the land of Magog (Ezek. 38:1-3) are today found in the geographical confines of Russia.

to be fulfilled, the prophecies declaring the restoration of Israel would have to be in the process of fulfillment. Today's generation is the only one that has seen a birth of Israel since the Babylonian captivity of 606 B.C. Israel's existence today means the stage is set for the attempted invasion of Israel by Russia.

God spoke through Ezekiel concerning Russia: *I will turn thee back, and put hooks into thy jaws, and I will bring thee forth, and all thine army, horses and horsemen, all of them clothed with all sorts of armour, even a great company with bucklers and shields, all of them handling swords* (v. 4).

You may ask, "Do you believe that Russia will come against Israel on horseback?" Of course not. If we were living in Ezekiel's day, I would say, "Yes," but we aren't. Remember that in Ezekiel's day the best means for transporting armies was the horse. But we don't use the horse today. We use fast-moving, powerful, mechanized equipment (such as the tank). This has taken the place of the horse.

Someone may ask, "Haven't you read that Russia is purchasing horses from all over the world?" Yes, I have. In attempting to verify that rumor, I have found that it is totally without support. Russia is not buying horses from all over the world. She is turning out tanks at the greatest rate of any nation in all of history. Today Russia has approximately 80 thousand tanks while the United States has only about 15 thousand.

Why do I believe that Russia's initial attack on Israel will be airborne? Examine the following verse in which Ezekiel by inspiration of the Holy Spirit describes this action: *Thou shalt ascend and come like a storm, thou shalt be like a cloud to cover the land, thou, and all thy bands, and many people with thee* (v. 9).

This scripture clearly describes an attack from the air. If you ascend, you get airborne. If you come like a storm, you come out of the heavens as a storm does. If you are like a cloud to cover the land, you come from the skies. This verse describes an airborne strike using a rapid deployment force, a tactic involving transport planes which can move complete armies quickly.

Russia has demonstrated an expertly developed rapid deployment ability. The world saw it when Russia invaded Afghanistan and again when, in only ten hours, she moved three combined armies from her Black Sea bases into Ethiopia in November of 1977. There can be no question that Ezekiel was describing Russia's military strategy to move armies by air, not horseback.

Will the military hardware mentioned in Ezekiel 39 be made of lignastone which burns slowly like coal?

The answer is, *No!* Lignastone, made by an old European process, is similar to laminated wood. It does have a greater tensile strength than steel, and it will burn. However, all Russian military equipment such as tanks, artillery, trucks, and guns are made of the finest Russian steel. (I have had the opportunity of examining captured Russian equipment.)

One's understanding would be enlightened upon carefully reading Ezekiel 39. If Russia were still using wooden bows, arrows, and spears, then these weapons would burn. However, in our modern period of advanced warfare, weapons are propelled by several types of fuel. This is the fuel the Israelis will capture which gives them a seven-year supply.

Ezekiel 39:6 states: *I will send a fire on Magog, and among them that dwell carelessly in the isles: and they shall know that I am the Lord.* **What is your interpretation of this scripture?**

Magog, the great land area north of Israel that will threaten the new nation of Israel, is Russia. When some evil force moves to destroy a people who are His, God has one alternative. To spare His own, He will allow the evil force to be destroyed.

The action described in the above verse constitutes a complete destruction of Russia, including her entire coast. (The word *isles* is better interpreted as ''coastlands.'')

God is saying, ''I will cause nuclear explosions over the land of Russia and her coastlands.'' Since this action is a direct intervention of God to save Israel, God may add His own brand of fire and brimstone to the nuclear blasts.

Where does the United States appear in Bible prophecy?

We find reference to the United States in Ezekiel 38:13. This scripture speaks of *the merchants of Tarshish, with all the young lions thereof.* The merchants of Tarshish represented the empires of Ezekiel's day. The merchants of that time exchanged their goods at the Mediterranean port of Tarshish.

With the fall of Rome, the empire system also collapsed, bringing about the next system: the colonial powers. The major colonial powers were England, France, Spain, Italy, and Portugal. Of these, England created an empire so vast that the sun never set on the British Empire.

The symbol of England then and now is a lion. Therefore, the "young lions" would be the offspring of England: Australia, Canada, New Zealand, South Africa, and the United States.

When Russia thinks to come against the new state of Israel, as described in Ezekiel 38:13, the United States is one of the "young lions" which comes to Israel's aid. The United States in prophecy is the sponsor of Israel—a divine assignment. And as long as she remains the major sponsor of Israel, the blessings of God will remain on her. (Gen. 12:3.)

Will America suffer war? Some "prophets" have said the United States will be severely persecuted and attacked by Russia, Japan, and China. Is there any biblical basis for this?

The answer to the last question is an absolute *No!* In no way does prophecy indicate that the United States will be severely persecuted by China or Japan.

In answer to the first question, there will be no war for America until she helps defend Israel against Russia. (Ezek. 38 and 39.) At that time, Russia will be destroyed by God with the help of the United States, one of the young lions. (Ezek. 38:13.) America, however, will neither lose a man nor suffer any destruction.

Do you believe that Christians should stockpile food and goods?

I am aware of some ministers who teach that Christians should stockpile food and water because the Church is going into a very dark hour. Let's examine what the Word of God has to say.

The Psalmist says, *I have not seen the righteous forsaken, nor his seed begging bread* (Ps. 37:25). (See also Ps. 34:1-10 and the words of Jesus in Matt. 6:25-34 for assurance that our physical needs are supplied.) Furthermore, the Old Testament reveals that when the righteous prophets went into an area where there was famine, they took no food with them. What little food there was got blessed. Because the people shared food with the prophet, it never ran out again.*

The Word of God prophesies famine, but not worldwide famine. The only nations presently self-sufficient in

---

*As one example, see the account of Elijah and the widow in 1 Kings 17:10-15. When the widow gave Elijah some of her last cake, as he told her to do, *She, and he, and her house, did eat many days* (v. 15).

food production are Israel, the United States, Canada, Australia, New Zealand, and the Republic of South Africa. These nations are not only self-sufficient, but producing more food than their people need. As I discussed previously, these are the five nations prophesied to be the sponsors of Israel. Because they are, the blessings of God are upon them. (Gen. 12:3.)

Is it possible that the United States is the New Israel and the present-day Jews are Zionists?

By no stretch of the imagination can the United States be identified as the New Israel. Some of this teaching stems from the error of British-Israel doctrine.* Upon studying the Old

---

*The doctrine of British/Israel has been around for a long time. It is a belief that the Anglo-Saxon races are descendants of the ten northern tribes of Israel. The teachers of this material claim that the ten tribes were lost following Assyrian captivity. However, when one studies Ezekiel, chapter 36, he discovers that God places the *whole* house of Israel back upon the land. (Ezek. 36:24.) So how could they have been lost?

Testament prophecies, one can make no mistake in discovering that God's plan is to restore the true nation of Israel in its Middle Eastern location.

Many modern Jews are Zionists. Zionism was founded before the turn of the century by Theodor Herzl. The movement involves both Jews and Gentiles who are dedicated to restoring geographically the national homeland of the Jews. This, by the way, is the will of God.

What position should a born-again man or woman of draft age take regarding the draft issue?

First of all, because the President of the United States has not called for the draft, there is no draft issue. If Russia were to continue gobbling up nation after nation, the United States would eventually have to take some military action. Therefore, the President has asked for a registration of our youth, 19 and 20 years old.

If I were a young man, 19 or 20 years old, I would do what the Scriptures tell me to do: I would obey the laws of the land. (Tit. 3:1.) I would register for the draft. Should the world situation present a crisis requiring me to be drafted into the military, I would serve as a good American. I include this question in this book because future wars are prophesied.

Who is the army of 200 million and where is it going?

Revelation 9:13-21 and 16:12,16 clearly describe this army. It is led by the kings of the East (from this we know that it is Oriental) and is moving westward for one year before arriving at the Valley of Megiddo, its destination being the Battle of Armageddon.

The Bible says there shall be a way made for the kings of the East. What does this mean? Is "the way" a highway from China to Israel?

Revelation 16 tells us that the River Euphrates will be dry, permitting the kings of the East (the Orientals) to cross into Israel. (v. 12.) They are on their way to Armageddon. (v. 16.) The 200 million-man Oriental army, led by its kings and driven by demons, will have moved through and destroyed the most populated area of the world before arriving at the Euphrates. (See Rev. 9:13-21 for additional information.)

Are World War III and the Battle of Armageddon the same?

No, indeed. Ezekiel 38 and 39 describe World War III; Zechariah 14 and Revelation 14, 16, and 19 describe the Battle of Armageddon.

Upon careful examination of these scriptures, you will discover that the battle sites are not the same. World War III is fought in the mountains north of Israel, while the Battle of Armageddon is fought in the Valley of Megiddo which stretches out into the plains of the Valley of Jezreel. These scriptures also reveal that neither the opponents nor the outcomes are the same. Furthermore, from Ezekiel 39 we learn that there is a seven-year period between these two battles.

Are there two Armageddons: one at the end of the Tribulation and one at the end of the Millennium?

At the end of the Millennium, Satan is released for a little season. (Rev. 20:7.) He gets a following of people from the earth, referred to as Gog and Magog (v. 8), though it is not the same Gog and Magog of Ezekiel 38 and 39 which identifies Russia.

Satan takes this following against the camp of the Saints at Jerusalem. This event is not really a war for God uses supernatural fire to consume the company on the spot, then casts Satan into the lake of fire. (vv. 9,10.)

The Battle of Armageddon occurs at the very end of the Tribulation. So you can see that the Battle of Armageddon is not the same as the situation that occurs at the end of the Millennium.

What weapons will be used in the Battle of Armageddon?

After one examines Zechariah 14 and Revelation 19, it becomes apparent that the forces of the Antichrist and the huge Oriental army will have tremendous fire power of a nuclear nature.

When the Antichrist and the Oriental army oppose Jesus, He uses the Word against them. (Rev. 19:15.) The Word releases a physical plague. Some people have described the effects of this plague to be the same as those caused by a neutron bomb.

And this shall be the plague wherewith the Lord will smite all the people that have fought against Jerusalem; Their flesh shall consume away while they stand upon their feet, and their eyes shall consume away in their holes, and their tongue shall consume away in their mouth.

Zechariah 14:12

Remember, man obtained his knowledge to create destructive power from God. Therefore, God has at His disposal everything necessary to destroy men who are determined to harm Israel.

Does Satan have access to the throne of God? Is he still the accuser of the brethren?

Recall that Lucifer (Satan) rebelled against God. From the Scriptures, we are certain that Satan lost in his attempt to unseat God and was cast out of heaven by Michael and his angels. (Is. 14:12-20; Rev. 12:7-9.)

We can understand when this happened by connecting Isaiah's account of the destruction Satan caused (ch. 14) with Jesus' statement in the Gospel of Luke: *I beheld Satan as lightning fall from heaven* (Luke 10:18). Since there is no biblical record of Satan having accomplished such destruction in the past and no statements prophesying a future destruction of the magnitude Isaiah describes, Satan's fall from heaven can be placed in only one spot. That location is in the time frame between Genesis 1:1 and Genesis 1:2.

We know God never creates anything and leaves it in the condition described in Genesis 1:2. It says, *The earth was without form, and void; and darkness was upon the face of the deep.* The destruction referred to by Isaiah occurred at the time that Satan lost his battle and was cast out of heaven. Satan all but destroyed the earth, but God then recreated His handiwork in six days and created man, to whom He gave total power and authority.

Remember, Jesus told His disciples that He saw Satan fall from heaven. Therefore, Satan's fall had to occur prior to Jesus' coming to earth as our Savior.

Do not allow anyone to confuse you about the time sequence simply because the battle between Satan and Michael the Archangel is described in The Revelation. One must keep in mind that this book is God's final chapter—the last act, the grand finale—of His masterwork in which He puts the whole picture together. Satan was cast out of heaven long ago. He does *not* have any access to the throne of God.

God has declared Satan to be a liar in whom there is no truth. (John 8:44.) Knowing that such a person would be lying absolutely, God would never give him any audience.

Satan *is* the accuser of the brethren. His initial accusations were against other angels, his brothers. Now he can only accuse you and me. But not to God! He accuses us to one another and to ourselves. By his accusations, he manages to separate us or keep us in self-condemnation. Either way, he short-circuits the believer who will listen to him.

Note: Do not allow the story in the first chapter of Job to confuse you. Verse 6

111

says, *Now there was a day when the sons of God came to present themselves before the Lord, and Satan came also among them.* Upon carefully reading the rest of the account, you will discover that the scene did not take place in heaven. Job and the men were assembled on earth where God gave them an audience. Earthlings could not appear before the throne, nor could Satan.

Where do dinosaurs and cavemen fit into Bible prophecy?

As previously mentioned, careful study of Genesis, chapter 1, reveals quite a gap between the first and second verses:

In the beginning God created the heaven and the earth.

And the earth was without form, and void; and darkness was upon the face of the deep.

We know that since God did not create this planet in the condition

112

described in verse 2, something very cataclysmic had to have occurred.

Isaiah 14:12-20 gives the account of the destruction that Lucifer (Satan) caused when he was defeated by the archangel Michael, then cast out of heaven. The remains of dinosaurs and prehistoric men give proof of an existence before Satan's fall. It is also possible that some species may have become extinct by the time of the Flood.

What part did the Holocaust of World War II play in the Bible?

During World War I, the British Parliament created a legal document called the Balfour Agreement which returned a partitioned area of ancient Israel to the Jews. The Zionists, overjoyed, began the development of agricultural centers. As a whole, however, the Jewish people were not excited about the gift. Not until the Holocaust of World War II did the Jews begin the official biblical return.

God allows both good and bad events to occur in order to cause prophetic events to be fulfilled within His timetable. Since the Israelis resisted the will of God for them to return to ancient Israel, it took a very severe event to send them home. Ezekiel 37 gives the biblical account.

In the Old Testament adultery is referred to as idolatry. Concerning the Jewish male virgins, is it possible that the Bible refers not to sex but to the worship of false gods?

I think not. Revelation 14:1-5 clearly and specifically tells us that these 144,000 have not married or had illicit relationships.

How will the 144,000 be sealed?

The sealing of the 144,000 Jewish evangelists takes place in Jerusalem around the temple mound. They will be sealed in their foreheads. Ezekiel 9 and Revelation 7 describe the event. The act of sealing is carried out by an angel. They are the first ones to be saved after the catching up of the Church, thus they are the firstfruits of that period. (Rev. 14:4.)

Will the city of Babylon be rebuilt, or can the reference in Revelation 18 be to some existing city?

Rumors that Babylon is presently being rebuilt are unsupported. Some excavations are being made, but only in an attempt to create a tourist attraction. Nothing in the Scriptures convinces me that the actual city of Babylon will be rebuilt.

From the information set forth in The Revelation, I find that Geneva, Switzerland, fits the description better than any other city now existing. Geneva is a sort of world capital. Nations create treaties there. Also, Geneva houses the headquarters of the World Bank and the World Council of Churches.

115

It seems as if the plagues of Revelation, chapter 9, are intended to bring men to repentance. Is this true?

Verses 20 and 21 of Revelation 9 state:

The rest of the men which were not killed by these plagues yet repented not of the works of their hands, that they should not worship devils, and idols of gold, and silver, and brass, and stone, and of wood: which neither can see, nor hear, nor walk:

Neither repented they of their murders, nor of their sorceries, nor of their fornication, nor of their thefts.

Repentance comes only by believing the Gospel and accepting Jesus as Savior. The plagues referred to in the above passage are designed to hinder the Antichrist and his plan while also serving as an awful consequence for blaspheming God.

Will all the born-again Christians stand before the Great White Throne

Judgment of Revelation 20 or will it be just the unsaved?

The righteous of all ages will stand before the Great White Throne Judgment, but not to be judged. The wicked will be judged, while the righteous will only be present. However, 1 Corinthians 6:2-4 tells us that the saints will judge both the world and the angels. This presents the possibility that the Church may be part of the Judge at the White Throne Judgment.

How do you get your name written in the Book of Life?

Jesus said, *Go ye into all the world, and preach the gospel* (good tidings) *to every creature. He that believeth and is baptized shall be saved; but he that believeth not shall be damned* (Mark 16:15,16). When a person accepts Jesus as Savior and Lord, he becomes a new creature and his name goes into the Book of Life. (2 Cor. 5:17.)

Do you equate the satellites which broadcast Christian TV programs with the angels that preach the Gospel in loud voices, mentioned in Revelation 14:6-11?

Indeed not! Were satellites the same as angels, all angels would be nothing more than pieces of machinery. Furthermore, the ministry originates with the angel, not with a satellite. Satellites can be controlled and turned off; angels have unlimited ability. We must cease this type of speculation and start believing and saying only what the Scriptures say.

Are we in the midst of revival?

The falling away occurring right now along with the outpouring of the Holy Spirit is creating a spiritual awakening.

Presently, the Holy Spirit is doing a tremendous job of rekindling spiritual fires within the hearts of the people everywhere. More and more people who once walked closely with the Lord are in the process of returning. That is very exciting!

Think about it for a moment: If everybody who has ever come to know Jesus Christ as personal Savior would get back into fellowship with Him and other believers, none of our churches would be big enough to house the crowd!

Yes, I believe revival is the order of the day.

Conclusion

My intention in writing this book has not been to answer every question concerning prophecy and revelation. However, my staff and I felt it would be an aid to the serious Bible student, as well as one just beginning the study of the Holy Scriptures.

There is certainly a possibility that a number of other questions on this subject can and should be raised. As you study the prophetic books and encounter questions for which no answers appear, please take time to write them down and send them to me. I would like to produce a second volume of *Questions and Answers on Bible Prophecy* in the future.

May God continue to increase your understanding of His Word as you study.

—Hilton Sutton

Subject Index

Subject Index

Subject Index

125

Subject Index

Subject Index

Subject Index

Subject Index

Scripture Index

Books of the Bible are arranged alphabetically disregarding the numeral when one appears at the beginning of the title.

The order of listing is as follows: book, chapter, verse. Page numbers following the entries are italicized.

Scripture Index

Ephesians
  ch. 4,*61*
    vv. 11-15,*35,82*
    v. 16,*17,35,82*
  ch. 5
    v. 27,*19,57,82*
Ezekiel
  ch. 9,*114*
  ch. 36,*103*
    v. 24,*103*
  ch. 37,*114*
  ch. 38,*94,101,106,107*
    vv. 1-3,*94*
    v. 4,*95*
    v. 9,*96*
    v. 13,*99-101*
  ch. 39,*94,97,98,101,106,107*
    v. 6,*98*
Genesis
  ch. 1,*112*
    v. 1,*110,112*
    v. 2,*110,112,113*
  ch. 5
    v. 24,*23*
  ch. 12
    v. 3,*44,66,101,103*
Hebrews
  ch. 1
    vv. 13-14,*59*
  ch. 2
    v. 14,*51*
  ch. 9
    v. 27,*26*
    v. 28,*11,20,23*
  ch. 11
    v. 5,*23*
Hosea
  ch. 6
    vv. 1-3,*86*
Isaiah
  ch. 2
    v. 2,*82*

Isaiah *(Continued)*
    v. 4,*84*
  ch. 11,*61*
    vv. 5-9,*47*
  ch. 14
    vv. 12-20,*109,113*
  ch. 19,*78*
    vv. 23-25,*45,48*
  ch. 42
    v. 1,*55*
  ch. 45
    v. 4,*55,*
  ch. 65
    v. 9,*55*
Job
  ch. 1
    v. 6,*111*
Joel
  ch. 2
    vv. 28-29,*85*
John
  ch. 6
    v. 44,*16*
  ch. 8
    v. 44,*111*
  ch. 13
    vv. 34-35,*82*
  ch. 14
    v. 3,*8,12,23*
  ch. 15
    v. 26,*16*
  ch. 16
    v. 8,*16*
  ch. 17
    v. 21,*34*
  ch. 20
    vv. 16-17,*50*
1 John
  ch. 2
    vv. 18-19,22,*70*
  ch. 3
    v. 2,*50*

Scripture Index

Scripture Index

Scripture Index

Hilton Sutton is regarded by many as the nation's foremost authority on Bible prophecy as related to current events and world affairs.

As an ordained minister of the Gospel, Dr. Sutton served as pastor for several years before being led out into the evangelistic field. Today he travels throughout the world, teaching and preaching the Word. He takes the words of the most accurate news report ever—the Word of God—and relates it to the news today.

Having spent over twenty years researching and studying the book of Revelation, Hilton Sutton explains Bible prophecy and world affairs to the people in a way that is clear, concise, and easy to understand. He presents his messages on a layman's level and shows the Bible to be the most accurate, up-to-date book ever written.

Hilton Sutton and his family make their home in Humble, Texas, where he serves as chairman of the board of *Mission To America*, a Christian organization dedicated to carrying the Gospel of Jesus Christ to the world.

For a complete list of books
and tapes by Hilton Sutton
or to receive his monthly
publication, UPDATE, write:

Mission To America
736 Wilson Road
Humble, TX 77338

WORLD WAR III

God's Conquest of Russia

Historic Fulfillment of God's Word

Bible prophecy allows you literally to observe God keeping His Word.

- More than 2600 years ago, God spoke through His prophet Ezekiel and told of the rise of Russia and its threat to the security of Israel.

- All eyes turn to the Middle East as the world follows a collision course with destiny. Israel lies at the center of the most strategic military spot on planet Earth.

- Both Russia and China are set for world conquest. Learn what is ahead for these two in a major military confrontation.

Hilton Sutton unfolds the prophecies of the Old and New Testaments. He brings you to an awareness that the events you are watching today are leading to the greatest climax of history that our world will ever know.

HARRISON HOUSE

P.O. Box 35035 • Tulsa, OK 74135

THE BEAST SYSTEM
Europe In Prophecy

"This book was written to unfold the Holy Spirit's definition of the Beast, when it will be revealed and its effects on the world. You'll read about Satan's secret plans to take over the entire world, and the Church's devastating impact on this plan."

YOU WILL LEARN ABOUT:
The Antichrist
The Mark of the Beast — 666
The Beast System's Control
Armageddon
The European Common Market

Hilton Sutton's teaching has freed many believers to receive the Bible as the most accurate, up-to-date book ever written. Although relating biblical prophecy to today's world has long been considered a controversial issue, Rev. Sutton's research and study of the Word has produced a clear, concise, and easy-to-understand book on the end-time.

HARRISON HOUSE
P.O. Box 35035 • Tulsa, OK 74135